Heartfelt Poems

of

Mine

(My Beginning)

Patricia L. Brown
Clinton, MD

Heartfelt Poems
Copyright © 2015 by Patricia L. Brown

All Scriptures are taken from the King James Version of the Bible.

All rights reserved under International Copyright Law. No part of this book may be reproduced or transmitted in any form or by any means without written permission of the Publisher, except for the inclusion of brief quotations in a review.

Published by:
Patricia L. Brown
Clinton, Maryland

Published in the United States of America.

ISBN 978-0-692-52698-9

Dedication

In Loving Memory

I want to dedicate this book to my immediate family members who have gone home to be with the Lord:

My loving father Emanuel, who died from complications of pneumonia in 1995. I love and miss him so much. I often *seriously* joke with my sisters from time to time saying, "I was daddy's favorite." I believe that I was, but of course it starts a friendly debate!

To my loving sister Felecia; her husband, my loving brother-in-law Gene; their daughter, my sweet loving niece Brittany; and their son, my loving nephew Trey. The entire family was tragically killed by a drunk driver one Saturday night in 2003 on their way home from a day of shopping and dining. This accident just happened to occur right in front of our hometown church.

To my loving mother Shirley, also known to most people as "Granny," who died from complications of Alzheimer's disease in 2012. I so wanted to share all of my successful accomplishments with my mother; however, I procrastinated so long before I took the time to write this book. I dedicate it in her memory.

And to my dear sweet sister Sheila, who died in 2013 from complications related to colon cancer. Sheila is the one sister that I teased the most and I miss her a lot. I used to love to see her face when I drew her name at Christmas time and when I gave her gift to her. I would sometimes hide money somewhere in her gift for her to find. She would always ask me for my old pocketbooks and each time I gave her one, I would hide money in each compartment for her to find. What blessed my heart was the expressions of joy on her face each time she found a $10 dollar bill, a $5 dollar bill, and especially a $20 dollar bill! It's always a blessing to bless someone else.

Acknowledgement

I first want to acknowledge the closest members of my family in my life today: my children Renita and Charles, Jr.; my grandchildren: Daija, Daijon and Vernon, Jr.; my sisters: Arnita, Brenda, Mary, Cathy, Bridget, and Jamie. I love you all and we are all that we have left, with God as our Heavenly Father to guide us.

While my sisters and I no longer have our earthly parents with us, we are blessed to have a huge family of cousins and we truly love each other. Our love is especially shown when we all get together and have fun at our family cook-outs, enjoy a family member's wedding, and sorrowfully and inevitably at a homegoing service.

Table of Content

Preface 13

Our Heavenly Father 15
    I Love the Lord 17
    God Made This World 18
    Think and Seek 20

Friendship 23
    Kind Words from a Friend 25
    Hearing Your Voice as you Recover 26
    Follow Your Dreams Today 28
    Missed Your Party 29
    To a Friend at Church 30
    The Soiree 31
    Thanks for Checking on Me 32

Happy Birthday 33
    A Birthday Thank You 35
    Eighty Years of Life 36
    A Silly Happy Birthday Wish for Cathy 37
    A Birthday Wish to Sister Bren 38
    Happy Birthday Ms. Florine 39

Sense of Humor 41
    I Like It When 43
    It's a New Day and a New Time 45

    Don't Forget to Pay Your Taxes 46
    Stop Acting Like … 48
    Why Are You So Hard-Headed? 50

Retirement 53
    On Your Retirement 55

Co-worker Farewell 57
    Major Milestone 59

Prayers 61
    I Asked God to Protect You 63
    That Peace 65
    Sheila's Health Challenge 66

Job Promotion 69
    Congratulations on Your Promotion 71

Thank You 73
    I Ate and the Food was Great 75

Love Poems 77
    Why Do I Hold On? 79

Happy Boss' Day 81
    Happy Boss Day Card 83

With Sincere Sympathy 85
    With Sincere Sympathy During Your Loss 87
    A Sympathy Card, I Sent to a Friend 88
    I Want to Comfort You 89

A Short Story 91
   I Spent A Day in the Life of a Pastor and His Wife 93
   We Spent a Day in the Life of a Pastor and His Wife 102

Notes 103

Contact Information 105

Preface

First and foremost I must give all honor and glory and all success in my life to my Lord and Saviour Jesus the Christ. Writing has been in my heart since I was a very young child. I truly believe that is one of the reasons God put me on this earth because He so patiently waited until I finally wrote what I am calling my *first* book.

When we were growing up, I used to watch my sisters read those thick *boring* novels, as I called them. I didn't like to read unless it was a short interesting story, so I decided to write my own short stories. I wrote what I felt in my heart, mostly fiction. I used to let one of my eight sisters read my stories to get her opinion and she always said she liked it; I hope she was being honest. Because she was always reading, I felt she would know a good book when she read it and that gave me more confidence. So much confidence that I somehow contacted a publishing company to request them to publish my short stories and to my surprise they responded. I was asked to meet the book publishing representative in Roanoke, Virginia, because that was the closest they would be coming to my small hometown. I had no way to get there and I never mentioned it to my parents. I knew we could not afford to travel to Roanoke because we were a large family with very little money. My mother and father had nine girls to raise and my father was the major breadwinner; working at the meat packing plant. My mom worked part time periodically. I knew they would not pay money for me to go to Roanoke *to take a chance*, so I had to get over it; however, I never forgot *that chance* I had to give up.

I still continued to write short stories over the years from time to time. I graduated from high school, enrolled in college, got married, moved to different locations over the years and lost practically everything that I wrote when I was growing up.

One of my co-workers once told me that if you don't use the gift that God gave you, He will take it from you and give it to someone else. That literally scared me to start getting more serious about finally becoming an author.

I hope that you will enjoy what I have written. I also hope that you will be inspired by at least one of my poems and enjoy my short story. They have been an inspiration to me and I pray that you will feel the same.

May God Bless You

Our

Heavenly

Father

I Love the Lord

*And thou shalt love the Lord
thy God with all thine heart,
and with all thy soul, and
with all thy might.*

Deuteronomy 6:5

I love the Lord, because He first loved me.
I can't do anything that He cannot see.

Because of His love, He gives me the freedom,
to do what I want and as I please.

But, I choose to serve Him and to live right.
Because He watches over me—
morning, noon and night.

He is my shepherd and your shepherd, too.
That's why it's not a good idea to do what you
want to do.

I love the Lord, because He first loved me.
I will live according to His Word, until
I'm lifeless and cannot breathe.

As I continue to learn what *Thus Saith the Lord,*
I yearn to serve Him more and more.

God Made This World

*And the Lord said unto Moses, How
long refuse ye to keep My
commandments and My laws?*

Exodus 16:28

God made this world, and didn't
need your help.
You corrupt it so bad, why are you
surprised that Jesus wept?

He gave you life, and said keep His
commandments, it all sounds easy,
but what's your intent?

Thou shalt not steal, but what do you do?
You do it any way and
go against His Will.

Thou shall not kill, but you take
a life, then get sentenced for
many long years.

Always tell the truth, do not lie,
especially in court when
you have to testify.

We all were born in sin,
but don't let sin win.
Let love motivate you
to just wake up, open up your eyes,
stop justifying what's corrupt.

Make the time that you have left
in this world good.
Seek the truth about God's
Word, go to church, make sure
the message is understood.

No matter what you have
done in your past,
You can turn your life around
and make it good, not bad.

Think and Seek

> *But seek ye first the Kingdom of God, and His righteousness; and all these things shall be added unto you.*
>
> **Matthew 6:33**

Think about your choices before you choose,
seek God's Word for guidance before you make
an investment and lose.

Think before you make a major decision.
Seek God for answers before your choice
causes a serious collision.

Think hard and be sensible, before you make an
expensive purchase.
Seek God for wisdom concerning your finances;
make sure it's in your budget;
and will not be a struggle.

Think before you make a hasty decision and
do something wrong.
You can't always recover, when some things are gone.

Remember once your choice is made, you don't
control the consequences.
They could be good, they could be bad, if you

don't seek God first, you will wish that you had.
Think about it before you tell a lie—to
your parents, to your teacher or on
your résumé.

Always tell the truth, or your parents will
punish you; your teacher will fail you; and
you could lose your job on your first day.

Friendship

Kind Words From a Friend

> *This is **My** commandment, that*
> *Ye love one another, as I*
> *have loved you.*
>
> **John 15:12**

'Just want to let you know how much I
appreciate
the phone calls I receive on an occasional day.

I remember one year while on vacation,
you called to check on me on my way to
the train station.

You had no special reason when you called me that
time.
Just wanted to let me know I was on your mind.

Just before you moved, you called me again,
Those few kind words mean a lot to a friend.

Hearing Your Voice as You Recover

Have mercy upon me, O Lord;
for I am weak: O Lord, heal me;
for my bones are vexed.

Psalm 6:2

First, I want to say, it is always great to
hear your voice, each and every time that
I call.

God, with His awesome healing powers, is a
Blessing and Deliverer to us all.

I'm so glad that He loves us unconditionally,
And hear our prayers when we fall on bending knee.

Some days we may be better than others;
But each and every day, we know that God
still loves us.

When I call you, I'm calling for us all,
to give well wishes from your church
family, co-workers and the
people living down the hall.

Although you are recovering and we're
wishing you well,
With the kindness in your heart, you're
still keeping us in your prayers.

I thank God for His love and for being my teacher.
I asked Him to protect you, when I cannot
reach you.

Follow Your Dreams Today

*Let us therefore follow after
the things which make for peace, and
things wherewith one may edify another.*

Romans 14:19

Follow your dreams today,
please don't procrastinate;
'Cause tomorrow, just may be
one day, too late.

Now there may be times,
your future may look dense,
But, don't decline, just have
a lot of con-fi-dence.

You know what's in your heart,
so, please do not stop;
until you are fulfilled with some
of life's thrills.

Your accomplishments just may be,
more than a blessing to thee.
Make this your new beginning, be
successful, keep on winning!

Don't think twice, follow your
dreams today, please don't be
a person who procrastinate.

Missed Your Party

> *Every good gift and every perfect gift is from above, and cometh from the Father of lights, with whom is no variableness, neither showdown of turning.*
>
> **James 1:17**

Birthday's to me are very dear;
it's a blessing to live and see another year.

You can't take it lightly, so blessed to be;
with friends, co-workers and your
entire family.

I'm sorry to say that I'm too busy today,
I can't bring you a gift, I have to
work the night shift.

May God Bless you, as you celebrate;
with good food, lots of fun on
your special day.

I'm sorry that I missed your party,
I'm sure it was a lot of fun,
a great big jubilee.

To a Friend at Church

> *Withhold not good from them to whom it is due, when it is in the power of thine hand to do it.*
>
> **Proverbs 3:27**

Thank you my friend for my lovely birthday card.

Just knowing you remembered, so warmed my heart.

I thank God for letting me see yet another year.

And for sending me friends that are so friendly
and so dear.

Those kind words you say on Sunday's mean a lot.

Just know that I care and I love you back!

May God continue to Bless you,
Bless your husband and your
children, too.

The Soiree

> *And the second is like, namely this,*
> *THOU SHALT LOVE THY NEIGHBOR*
> *AS THYSELF. There is none other*
> *commandment greater than these.*
>
> **Mark 12:31**

I know it's been about 30 days,
since I visited your home to attend
"The Soiree."

I know this is long overdue; I had planned
to send it in a day or two.

But, even though my card is late; you
must know that the food was great.

The music was on time! Our pictures look fine.
I think we all had a really good time.

So, thanks so much for inviting me and
giving me my personal DVD.

Thanks for Checking on Me

> *A man that hath friends*
> *must show himself friendly:*
> *and there is a friend that*
> *sticketh closer than a brother.*
>
> **Proverbs 18:24**

I just want to let you know, how much I
appreciate the phone calls
that I received on a non-occasion day.

Your friendship's so real,
I can remember the year I received
a call from you while on vacation;
that call did my heart good just to know,
I was on your mind during that time.

And just before you moved,
you called me again, those
kind words mean a lot to a friend.

Sometimes I get so busy and
I don't remember,
To send you a note or
dial your number.

I have to thank you so much
for being so kind,
and checking on me from
time to time.

HAPPY

BIRTHDAY

A Birthday Thank You

*A friend loveth at all times, and
a brother is born for adversity.*

Proverbs 17:17

I just want to thank you for thinking of me,
when I celebrated my birthday, just last week.

It was a beautiful card, but more than that,
you have been a good friend from the time
that we met.

You have a kind heart and have blessed me in
many ways.
your smile, your phone calls, just the things
that you say.

May God continue to Bless you and
your family, too.

Because you Bless me as a friend, with your
sincere cards and calls to say I love you.

Eighty Years of Life

*For length of days, and long
life, and peace, shall
they add to thee.*

Proverbs 3:2

Even though you may not know me,
since we have never met.

I consider it an honor to be invited
with your other special guest.

You have reached a major milestone to
celebrate 80 years.

It's the same age my mother would be,
if she had only lived.

May God continue to bless you to live a
long, long time.

I hope to get another invitation,
when you reach age 99.

A Silly Happy Birthday Wish for Cathy

> *And he humbled thee, and suffered thee to hunger, and fed thee with manna, which thou knewest not, neither did thy fathers know; that he might make thee know that man doth not live by bread only, but by every word that proceedeth out of the mouth of the Lord doth man live.*
>
> **Deuteronomy 8:3**

On the front of your card, you'll
see a paper cake.
For it is the kind that I rather bake.

No sugar, no flour, no vanilla extract,
I don't have to worry about
measuring exact.

So get a pair of scissors and cut out
your paper cake.
Slice it in pieces and give your sisters
a taste.

My birthday wish was silly and I hope you
got a laugh,
A paper cake this year, maybe next
year paper cash!

A Birthday Wish to Sister Bren

*There is gold, and a multitude of
rubies: but the lips of knowledge
are a precious jewel.*

Proverbs 20:15

I am sending you these diamonds instead
of a cake,
To show you how special you are and to
say Happy Birthday.

We are all that we have left here in this world,
No parents, no grandparents, just us girls.

So enjoy these special gems that I send to you,
"Sparkling" diamonds—a diamond ring,
and oh, a rose too!

Let me suggest that you go out to dinner,
or take some time out and go to a spa,
Just do something special on your 61st birthday.

But, don't go out alone, no matter what you decide,
take your sisters with you so you don't have
to pay.

Happy Birthday Ms. Florine

And it shall be our righteousness,
if we observe to do all these
commandments before the Lord
our God, as he hath commanded us.

Deuteronomy 6:25

Happy Birthday Ms. Florine, here is
a cake, now get yourself some ice cream!!

You are a woman after God's own heart, you
Praise Him whether you are in church or not.

You talk to the Lord on any given day,
you talk to Him at work and while you are
on your way.

It's always a blessing to live another year,
and thank our Lord and Savior that He kept you here.

May God Bless you on your special day, and
may you enjoy it in a righteous way.

Sense of Humor

I Like It When......

¹³Happy is the man that findeth wisdom, and the man that getteth understanding.

¹⁴For the merchandise of it is better than the merchandise of silver, and the gain thereof than fine gold.

Proverbs 3:13-14

I like it when I put on my coat for the
first time each year, and put my hand in
my pocket and find a crisp dollar bill.

I like it when I go to my mailbox
to get the mail, then open my box
and a check is in there.

I like it when I walk in the church
Sanctuary to get to my seat,
And sit on the same row, close
to the end each and every week.

I have to arrive at church by a certain time,
or that seat on the same row, close
to the end will not be mine.

I like it when I dress up and
go to the store, and

get 3 or 4 compliments as I
walk through the door.

I like waking up in the morning to
see the ground covered with snow,
then turn on the news to see
my agency is closed.

There are so many things I like,
so many I could name.
But, I'll just list a few for now,
maybe later I'll add more things.

It's a New Day and a New Time

Order my steps in thy word:
and let not any iniquity have
dominion over me.

Psalm 119:133

Always keep in mind, that everything
usually change with the time.

Even you will change, you won't
look the same.

Your black hair will become white,
your vision will get worse at night.

You might have 32 teeth now, oh
but wait and see,
you'll be hoping you can hold on to 23.

You are getting slower not walking the same,
even when you drive you stay in the slow lane.

Look at your face, not smooth anymore,
you are going to see things in the mirror
you never seen before.

If you don't get your life in order, you have
only you to blame.
There is more to life than social media
and playing video games.

Don't Forget to Pay Your Taxes

> *And the peace of God, which*
> *passeth all understanding, shall keep*
> *your hearts and minds through*
> *Christ Jesus.*
>
> **Philippians 4:7**

Don't forget to pay your taxes,
File your return early, get it
over so you can relax.

I know it gets you in a frenzy,
during that time, But, we all have
to do it, you file yours and I'll file mine.

I hope I don't have to pay,
I don't want to owe, I rather
break even, or receive a check, than to
give them a little bit of dough.

Put your life at ease, keep all of your receipts,
It will then-- be a breeze.
And if you end up having to pay,
do not fear, change your exemption,
so you'll get a check next year.

Sit down with your accountant to explore
your options, see if you need your money

during the year, to buy more food
and do some shopping.
So, don't forget tax time comes every year,
don't let them come after you, stop living in fear.

Stop Acting Like…….

*Now, my God, let, I beseech thee,
thine eyes be open, and let thine ears
be attent unto the prayer that is
made in this place.*

2 Chronicles 6:40

Stop acting like you can't live right,
as soon as someone look at you sideways,
you are ready to fight.

Stop acting like you can't fall on your knees
to pray before going to bed at night.
God don't care if your knees are crusty, looking
like they've been dip in flour all snowy and white.

He wants to reassure you that He will be there,
always there in your time of need.
It doesn't matter if you didn't put lotion on your knees.

Stop acting like you don't know what to say, you talk
to your other friends, talk to Him the same way.

So, if I were you and I am able, I'd say my
grace every time I sit at the table.

You can talk to Him while you are sitting, you
can talk to Him while you are standing.

With your sincere heart, talk to your Father,
He will never, ever think you are a bother.

He loves you with unconditional love,
You are His child, His dearly beloved.

Why Are You So Hard-Headed?
(When it comes to marriage)

> **Let the husband render unto the
> wife due benevolence: and likewise
> also the wife unto the husband.**
>
> **1 Corinthians 7:3**

Why do you take a vow and say 'til death do we part,
And don't try to make it work, with the person you
love with all of your heart?

When you somehow get the courage,
first seek God's Word, concerning marriage.

Talk to your Pastor, get counseling,
take pre-marital classes,
Do what it takes to make the
marriage last.

Life will be so much better, for you,
your husband and your children forever.

Your head is so hard, so determined to disobey,
why don't you take the institution of marriage
seriously? Get on your knees and pray.

Wife, love your husband, husband love your wife.
Stop being so hard-headed, just live

according to God's Word, choose life.
Then live forever and ever with your wife.

Stop being so hard-headed, open "the Book"
and read what it says.
Don't let anyone say, you had a very hard head.

Retirement

"On Your Retirement"

And from the age of fifty years they shall cease waiting upon the service thereof, and shall serve no more.

Numbers 8:25

Retiring from Federal Service is a major step to me;
the start of a new life, to relax and be at ease.

No more law cases to read, or documents to sign,
no catching public transit to get to work on time.

You will leave behind your huge workload;
no more privacy acts, freedom of information acts
or U.S. Codes.

From your early years, starting as a clerk,
to leaving the agency during a mass transfer.

You were a paralegal to the Counsel in 1979
and remained in that office, for the
remainder of your time.

We will surely miss you, being you are so kind,
But, just keep in mind—this is your time.

May God Bless you in all that you do,
even if it's nothing, it's what you choose.

Co-Worker Farewell

Major Milestone

And so it was, that, while they were there,
the days were accomplished
that she should be delivered.

Luke 2:6

What a major milestone, a big accomplishment,
I am so sorry that I missed the big event.

It was an honor to receive an invitation from you,
that was very kind of you to remember me, too.

You served your country in the Army for many years,
then became a Federal civilian
employee to further your career.

After being a soldier you didn't get tired,
you worked as a clerk, an administrator
and Evangelist on the side.

I still want to share in your retirement celebration,
so, here is a small token from me to show
my appreciation.

Prayers

I Asked God to Protect You

> *He shall cover thee with His feathers, and under His wings shalt thou trust: His truth shall be thy shield and buckler.*
>
> **Psalm 91:4**

I know I can't be around you 24 hours a day,
so I prayed and asked God to protect you
every step of the way.

As you go about your daily chores, or shopping
for food at the local stores.

He's watching over you, as I asked Him to.
Though I asked you to pray, that's something
you don't do.

It is God who makes sure all of your needs are met.
That's why I pray, 'cause you tend to forget.

He loves you unconditionally with all of His Heart,
I know you are aware, cause I tell you a lot.

I'm not just telling you to hear myself talk,
I want YOU to make an increase in your
Christian walk.

Let your friends know that Jesus is real,
He will protect them too; just as I asked
Him to protect you.

That Peace

> ***And the peace of God, which***
> ***passeth all understanding,***
> ***shall keep your hearts and***
> ***minds through Christ Jesus.***
>
> **Philippians 4:7**

That Peace, it's something you will never understand,

That Peace, is from someone more powerful than any man.

That Peace, His name is Jesus,

That Peace, try Him and you will see.

That Peace, will give you much joy,

That Peace, it's beyond belief.

That Peace that you feel within,

That Peace, when you are free from sin.

That Peace, that the Lord gives thee,

That Peace, keep it in your heart, don't let it go, don't let it leave.

Sheila's Health Challenge

*Fear thou not; for I am with thee:
be not dismayed; for I am thy God:
I will strengthen thee; yea, I will help
thee; yea, I will uphold thee with the
right hand of my righteousness.*

Isaiah 41:10

Dear God, I have a special prayer request for
my sister Sheila.
I need your healing powers to reign down
and heal her.

Lord, remove the affliction that's affecting her body,
Curse it at the root and let it all be forgotten.

Jesus you healed all the people of all
manner of sickness, all manner of disease.
I saw it in Your Word in Matthew 4:23

Her appetite was once strong, though,
now it is gone.

She used to desire plenty of food whenever she eats,
now her body lack nutrients, it is getting weak.
I trust you Lord, cause you know
what the outcome will be.

So, thank you Lord for all you have done,
after talking to you, I know her battle is
already won!

Job Promotion

"Congratulations on Your Promotion"

> *The Lord rewarded me according to my righteousness; according to the cleanness of my hands hath He recompensed me.*
>
> **Psalm 18:20**

Congratulations, so glad you were promoted.

It's good to see you moving up in your career,
but, I have to tell you, we're sure going to miss you around here.

It was wonderful working with a person that was nice and like-minded,
With a sincere Christian walk and treated people with kindness.

May God continue to Bless you in all of your endeavors,
And may you have peace and joy at <u>that</u> agency, another agency or—wherever.

Keep in touch with us and always remember, different people have different attitudes.
But, no matter how they may act, or what they may do.

Make sure you stay the way that you are, make sure that you, be you!

Thank You

I Ate and the Food Was Great

> *And he pressed upon them greatly;*
> *and they turned in unto him,*
> *and entered Into his house;*
> *and he made them a feast,*
> *and did bake unleavened*
> *bread, and they did eat.*
>
> **Genesis 19:3**

On Sunday, I had a wonderful time,
the conversation was good
and the food was great;
I'm so glad you invited me,
so glad I ate.

You are an excellent hostess,
which I am not.
But, maybe one day
I will give it a shot.

Thanks again, for being so kind,
Just wanted you to know
That I had a good time.

Love Poem

Why Do I Hold On?

> *A foolish woman is clamorous: she is simple, and knoweth nothing.*
>
> **Proverbs 9:13**

Why do I hold on, knowing
all hope is gone?

Why do I torture myself, knowing
there is no love left?

I know he doesn't care, he is not
a man that's willing to share.

All of this love, I mean a lot of love,
all of this love, between us.

I give him 100 percent and
he gives me 1 percent.

Why do I hold on, knowing
all hope is gone?

Still giving 100 percent, and
receiving 1 percent
knowing all along that it doesn't
make any sense.
Holding on keeps me depressed,

always under stress and can't
seem to get any rest.

He stays on my mind, I think
of him all the time.

But deep down I know, a future
with him just isn't so.

Don't know why I'm holding on,
knowing all hope is gone!!

Happy Boss' Day

Happy Boss' Day Card

Happy are thy men, happy are these thy servants, which stand continually before thee, and that hear thy wisdom.

1 Kings 10:8

This card and gift card do not describe in anyway, how grateful I am to have a great supervisor.

There is no employee that could ever ask for a better leader, friend or advisor.

This organization is better because of your leadership, I gained a lot of knowledge when you gave me a few history tips.

A brand name company that do not know you, can't say what a wonderful supervisor you are.

Because they don't know like I know, that you are the best boss by far.

With Sincere Sympathy

With Sincere Sympathy During Your Loss

*Precious in the sight of the Lord
is the death of his saints.*

Psalm 116:15

I received an e-mail recently, about the
loss of your brother.
I know how you feel and what you are going
through, because I recently loss my mother.

Please know that you and your family were on
my mind, in my thoughts and prayers
during that sad time.

No one can comfort you like our Lord and Saviour
Jesus Christ.
Just know that you have friends who care and prayed
for you each night.

The arrangements were in December and I
was not there.
I'm sending my love and want you to know,
how much I sincerely care.

A Sympathy Card I Sent to a Friend

> *Grace be to you and peace*
> *from God our Father, and from the*
> *Lord Jesus Christ.*
>
> **2 Corinthians 1:2**

Nothing is harder than losing someone
you love.

No matter the relation, no matter the kin,
it seems so hard, it just always does.

And even if you were not very close, that
family bond sure means the most.

I just want you to know that you are in
my prayers
Even if I don't say it, just know that I care.

I am your friend and send my sincere sympathy,
I'll be ever so near, if there is anything
that you need.

I Want to Comfort You

*Wherefore comfort one another
with these words.*

1 Thessalonians 4:18

I know comforting words cannot take away
the sadness in your heart.

But, there is a "Comforter" that can
guide you through any situation,
when others cannot.

I am sorry to hear about your tragedy;
but, being sorry cannot bring back
the son that you miss and need.

I send my deepest sympathy and
sincere love, to you and
to your family.

But, it's God's everlasting arms you
should lean on, during this
time of need!

A

Short Story

I Spent a Day in the Life Of a Pastor and His Wife

Jesus Is Lord!

The life of your Pastor and his wife is more than just seeing them on Sundays and mid-week Bible Study. Their lives are busier than we can imagine. On top of preparing a good message and presenting it to the congregation, there are more obligations, such as business matters, among other things that are done in the life of a Pastor. I had the blessed privilege to experience one *Day in the Life of a Pastor and his Wife*.

The days leading up to "the day" were more of excited anticipation. I was imagining how it would be, how will the plane look inside, what will I say, what will they say, will they like me, will I say or do something I should not say or do, will I embarrass myself or will I enjoy myself?

So many things were going through my mind leading up to that day. One thing I do know is that I couldn't wait; it was like getting ready to spend a day with the Holiest of Holiness and I wanted to be the perfect angel. I had an opportunity to be up close and personal with the people whose ministry literally changed my life. They taught me how to live a righteous life, what it really means to be saved and how to live according to God's Word. I often wonder how many other people in this world think the way I used to think; that as long as you go to church on Sundays you are a Christian and the people that don't go to church are the sinners. I grew up in church and quickly found out, once I heard the truth of God's Word simplified, that just going to church and not living according to God's Word after you leave the church does not make you a Christian.

This *day in the life of a Pastor and his wife* experience all started one night at a Christian School fund raising event. A few of my church friends and some people that became instant friends that night and I formed a group of six during that event. Our hearts were in it to donate money for a worthy cause and also earn a *day in the life of a Pastor and his wife*. The event itself was very exciting and a lot of fun. The fun and excitement was a gift in itself. Friendly competition. As it got down to the last two groups competing against each other, the excitement grew even more. When the winners were announced and it was our group, at that point it all became surreal.

After finding it hard to believe we were the winners, then posing for pictures, my first thought after that was that I was not dressed appropriately to be taking *"grand prize winner"* pictures. I certainly didn't consider myself camera-ready. But we were the grand prize winners and I was ecstatic! There were two things I used to imagine becoming a reality that night. First, I was going to ride on a private plane nicknamed "the fly mobile"; which was something I dreamed of doing when our church first purchased a plane many years ago. Second, I used to imagine what it was like to be on one of the many trips my Pastor and his wife used to tell the congregation about over the years. I wished that they would put together a video of all of their trips and schedule an event for members to eat popcorn and watch videos and pictures of some of the wonderful trips, see the people they visited and hear sermons taught at our other church locations, especially the ones in other countries. And, now I get to live both dreams, on *a day in the life of a Pastor and his wife.*

♡

Prior to the day of our departure, I received a call from my Pastor's wife and she asked me, "What size shoes do you wear?" I told her, she said thanks and that was the end of our conversation. I thought to myself, she's giving me a pair of shoes, too. "I can't wait!" We were never told where we were going. The instructions were to meet them at their lovely home on the morning of departure, and then we would travel in a motor coach to the hangar where "the fly mobile" is kept. I love surprises and enjoyed the excitement of not knowing where we were going until the plane landed.

The day finally arrived. I can't remember if I slept a wink the night before; I was too excited. That morning after I got dressed, I picked up one of the other members of our group and she was excited as well and we traveled to our Pastor's home. As we boarded the motor coach, we were greeted by our Pastor's wife, and she handed each of us a lovely gift; a pair of slippers with a matching bag monogrammed with our initials. (Thus, the reason for my shoe size.) After we all arrived and received our gifts, we started on our way. We were chauffeured by our Pastor. How often do you get the pleasure of being chauffeured by your Pastor? What a privilege and an honor.

There was also a photographer traveling with us to capture the moments of our trip the entire day. "So Formal"; it made me feel special. Of course, we all had our cameras and took personal pictures of special moments to share as well.

While we were traveling, our Pastor's wife prepared breakfast for us; she was such a gracious hostess. I often tell my friends that I am not a great hostess; however, on that day I thought, hmmm, I could learn from her. She gave us a quick tour of the motor coach. I'm not sure about any of my other friends but that was my first time seeing the inside of a motor coach or traveling on one. It is truly a mobile "home." A home—living room, kitchen, bedroom, bathroom, etc., and when it's parked, the living room and bedroom sections expand, or "bumps out," to add more living space. How cool was that! It made me want one and I don't even like to drive. It's gorgeous!!!

We finally arrived at the place (private airport, I call it) which houses the church plane. I learned that it is called a hangar, and we were then greeted by the friendly staff who boarded the motor home. And guess what? They gave each of us a gift; a gift bag filled with little goodies and a fruit basket for us all to enjoy, with a handwritten note that read:

Have a wonderful trip!
Enjoy the experience!
Best Regards & Blessings!

After the airport representative gave us the gift bag and the fruit, she told us to enjoy our trip to Georgia. She spoiled our surprise. We looked at each other and said, we are going to Atlanta. It was such a wonderful day. We were all so ecstatic. It didn't matter that we learned before we left where we were going instead of being surprised when we landed. We all exited the motor coach and then went inside to a waiting room, where we fellowshipped with each other, read magazines, and were offered coffee while we waited to board the plane.

The time finally arrived for us to board the plane. We went to the hangar and saw the plane. Nice!! There were also other planes inside that belonged to other churches, as well. We took a few pictures of our plane and I may have taken a few of the others.

We then boarded the plane, which was more than I expected. It was sooo clean! White "soft" seats! Gold fixtures! Gorgeous shiny brown paneling! It even had a Study Table! So no matter where this Pastor is, he studies the Word of God! Whether he is on dry land or thousands and thousands of feet in the air, he studies and prepares a *full gourmet meal* (or message) for his congregation. We never, ever get a carry-out snack from this Pastor!!

I was able to quickly get the seat that I wanted with a window, and the seat had a built in ottoman so I could prop up my feet. And if I knew what I was looking at, I could tell you approximately where we were in the air, with my little navigation-like system beside my seat. How do you like that! I decided right then and there, no more commercial planes for me; from now on I want to fly on a private jet. Well now, it seems like I was just joking. I meant it when I said it, but can't seem to make it a reality.

We all had a wonderful fellowship while flying, laughing and joking, taking pictures, eating; I don't think any of us went to sleep. We did take a tour of the plane; which is another "mini" home traveling in the air. My Pastor took each of us one by one in the cockpit to introduce us to the pilots and he explained the different things on the instrument panel to us. How educational.

We all learned a lot while traveling on the plane during our *day in the Life of a Pastor and his wife.* We asked them questions about God's Word, their ministry and other experiences in their lives over the years. We also shared how we each changed our lives and made a decision to live our lives according to God's Word to the best of our abilities and to just choose to stay converted. Some of us shared how we used to live our lives before we got saved; which can't compare to the amazing changes in our lives since we changed and turned our lives around. If you really give deep thought of how your life was before you got saved and the changes in your life and how you feel inside with God in your life, you will see what we mean and understand how we feel.

♡

    We landed in Georgia at a private airport and were greeted with waiting transportation to take us to the church in Atlanta. The weather was absolutely gorgeous on that day. As we arrived at the church, we snapped pictures of everything and everybody. We were greeted at the door by that Pastor and his wife. They welcomed us with such a friendly greeting and gave us a tour of the church. We saw the main sanctuary, as well as other rooms in the church. They also took us to the educational annex that was being remodeled. We ended up in the fellowship hall where we received more gifts, and they had a scrumptious meal prepared for us, complete with cooks and staff that waited on us. We felt like royalty! They made us feel at home. They also had a fancy menu printed for us at our table, which read something like this:

A Day in the Life of . . . . .

LUNCHEON

Monday, March 15, 2010

MENU

Chicken Marsala
Baked Tilapia
Rice Pilaf
Grilled Vegetables
Deluxe Salad
Dinner Rolls
Assorted Desserts
Iced Tea & Coffee Served

That food was so delicious that we asked for the recipes; which I later received in an e-mail from the chef.

The two Pastors conducted their official "Pastor's Business," and we tagged along experiencing *a day in the life of a Pastor and his wife*.

After the fun, food, fellowship, prayers and over enjoyment on such a lovely day, it was time to return home. We said our good-byes and headed back home; back to reality. The day was still surreal, but we were GOING HOME!!! I must say that the day wasn't long enough.

♡

We boarded the plane at the Atlanta airport and I took my favorite seat again. As we traveled, it was such a comfortable ride; no air pockets, no turbulence, just a smooth ride there and back. It really is the ONLY way to fly. Upon arrival back to the hangar, we boarded the motor coach, traveled back to our Pastor and his wife's home where our cars were parked. The trip didn't quite end there. We had an added attraction—a private tour of the Pastor and his wife's home. How do you like that!!! Needless to say, it was really lovely; the ambience made me feel at home. What a wonderful way to end a trip on *"a Day in the life of a Pastor and his wife."*

We Spent a Day in the Life
Of a Pastor and His Wife

> *So then*
> *neither is he that planteth any thing, neither*
> *he that watereth; but God*
> *that giveth the increase.*
>
> **1 Corinthians 3:7**

We spent a day in the life of *a Pastor and his wife*.
Trust me, we had a good time, I know I had
the time of my life.

The trip in itself just seemed surreal,
we all were so happy, almost in tears.

The trip originated because we gave a donation,
it was our heart's desire to further the
children's education.

All that we did was truly from our hearts.
We gave to the Christian School,
all together it was a lot.

It was well worth it and we thank God,
we had the resources.
And we'll do it all again, cause it's our
Heartfelt choices.

Notes

Notes

Contact Information

Patricia L. Brown
Clinton, Maryland

Email

PL54@juno.com